junie b. jones®
Has a Monster Under Her Bed

by BARBARA PARK

illustrated by
Denise Brunkus

Long tail Books

Junie B. Jones Has a Monster Under Her Bed by Barbara Park

This bilingual edition was published by Longtail Books in 2022 by arrangement with Barbara Park c/o Writers House LLC through KCC(Korea Copyright Center Inc.), Seoul.

ISBN 979-11-91343-15-1 14740

Longtail, Inc.

Contents

1
The Cheese Man

My name is Junie B. Jones. The B **stand**s **for** Beatrice. **Except** I don't like Beatrice. I just like B and **that's all**.

I am in the **grade** of afternoon **kindergarten**.

Today we got school pictures taken at that place.

School pictures is when you wear your bestest[1] dress. And you go to the

cafeteria. And a cheese man is there.

He makes you say *cheese*.[2] Only I don't actually know why.

Then he takes pictures of you. And your mother has to buy them. Or else you will get your feelings hurt.

School pictures is a **racket**, I think.

I wore my new dress with the **dinosaur** on the front.

"A dinosaur, huh?" said the cheese man.

I **smooth**ed my skirt very lovely.

"Yes," I said. "It is a Tyrannosaurus

---

1 **bestest** 단어 'best(최고의)'를 강조한 비격식적인 표현. '최고로 좋은'이라는 뜻을 나타내며 어린아이가 주로 사용한다. 이 책에 나오는 'worstest(worst)'도 이와 같은 경우이다.

2 **say cheese** 사진사가 사진을 찍을 때 사용하는 말. '치즈(cheese)'라고 말할 때 사람의 입이 웃는 모양이 되기 때문에 이 표현을 사용한다.

Dottie.[3]"

"You mean Tyrannosaurus *Rex,*" he said.

"No. I mean Tyrannosaurus Dottie. 'Cause Rex is the boy. And Dottie is the girl," I explained.

The cheese man stood behind his camera.

"Say *cheese,*" he told me.

"Yeah, only guess what? I don't actually know why I have to say that word. 'Cause what's cheese got to do with it?" I asked.

"Cheese makes you smile," said the cheese man.

I shook my head.

---

3 **Tyrannosaurus Dottie** 지상에 존재하였던 공룡 가운데 가장 강하다고 여겨지는 육식 공룡인 '티라노사우루스 렉스(Tyrannosaurus Rex)'에 주니 B.가 '도티(Dottie)'라는 여자 이름을 붙인 것.

"Not *me*. Cheese doesn't make *me* smile," I said. "'Cause sometimes I eat a cheese sandwich for lunch. And I don't even **giggle** when I **swallow** that thing."

The cheese man did a big breath.

"Could you please just say it?" he asked.

"Yes," I said. "I can *please just say it*. Only don't forget to tell me when you're ready. 'Cause one time my grampa[4] Frank Miller was taking my picture. And he didn't tell me he was ready. And then one of my eyes **turn**ed **out** opened. And the other one turned out closed."

I made the face to show him.

---

4 **grampa** '할아버지(grandpa)'를 부르는 말로, 'gramp', 'grampa', 'grampy' 등 다양한 표현이 있다.

"See? See my eyes? See how one of them is opened and the other one is . . ."

All of a sudden, the cheese man took my picture.

My mouth came wide open at him.

"HEY! HOW COME YOU DID THAT? HOW COME YOU TOOK MY PICTURE? 'CAUSE I WASN'T EVEN READY YET!"

The cheese man kept on **click**ing his camera.

Pretty soon he looked at the next person in line.

"Next," he said.

I **stamp**ed my foot.

"Yeah, only I wasn't ready, I tell you! And so I need another turn!" I said.

Just then, my teacher came over. And

she pulled me away from there.

She sat me next to her on a bench.

Her name is Mrs.

She has another name, too. But I just like Mrs. and that's all.

Mrs. said ***settle** down* to me.

Then me and her watched the rest of the children get their pictures taken.

My bestest friend named Lucille went next.

She had a blue satin[5] ribbon in her hair.

"My **nanna** says this ribbon **bring**s **out** the blue in my eyes," she told the cheese man.

She opened them real wide.

---

5 **satin** 새틴. 광택이 있고 매끄러운 천으로, 주로 장식적인 여성복, 핸드백, 모자 등에 사용된다.

"See them? See their color? They are robin's egg blue . . .[6] with just a ***hint*** of lavender.[7]"

The cheese man **suck**ed in his **cheek**s. He was getting **fusstration** in him, I think.

"Could you please just say *cheese*," he **grouch**ed.

Lucille smiled real big with all her teeth.

"Cheese!" she sang very loud. "Cheese! Cheese! Cheesie, cheese, cheese!"

Then she kept on singing *cheese*, till the cheese man said, "**Knock it off**."

---

6 **robin's egg blue** 로빈스 에그 블루. 지빠귀의 일종인 미국지빠귀(American robin)가 낳는 알의 색으로, 초록빛이 도는 청색인 청록색을 가리킨다.

7 **lavender** 보라색 꽃을 피우며 온 그루에 좋은 향기를 내는 식물인 라벤더의 꽃 색으로, 연한 보라색을 가리킨다.

After she was done, Lucille **skip**ped over to me and Mrs.

"Did you see me?" she asked. "Did you see how good I said *cheese?* That's because I'm going to be a model when I grow up. So I already know how."

She **fluff**ed her **fluffy** hair.

"The camera is my friend," she said.

Mrs. **roll**ed **her eyes** way up at the **ceiling**. I looked up there, too. But I didn't see anything.

After that, it was time for the class picture.

The class picture is when all of Room Nine lines up in two **row**s.

The biggie[8] kids stand in the back. And the shortie kids stand in the front.

I am a shortie kid. Only that is nothing to be **ashamed** of.

I stood next to Paulie Allen Puffer.

---

8 **biggie** 단어 'big(큰)'을 주니 B.가 'biggie'라고 장난스럽게 말한 표현. 이 책에 나오는 'shortie(short)', 'shakie(shake)', 'snarlie(snarl)' 등이 이와 같은 경우이다.

He looked very **admiring** at my dinosaur dress.

"Dinosaurs **bite** people's heads off," he said.

I did a **frown**.

"Yeah, only they don't even **scare** me. 'Cause there's no such things as dinosaurs anymore," I told him.

"So? There's still such things as **monster**s that can bite your head off," said Paulie Allen Puffer. "A monster lives right under your bed, I **bet**. My big brother says that *everybody* has a monster under their bed."

He **poke**d his finger at me.

"Even *you,* Junie B. Jones," he said.

I got **shiver**s on my arms.

"No, I do not either, Paulie Allen Puffer," I said.

"Yes, you do too," he said back. "My brother is in seventh grade. And he says the monster waits till you're asleep. Then he **crawl**s up next to you. And he lies down on your **pillow**. And he practices **fit**ting your head in his mouth."

I **cover**ed up my ears. But Paulie Allen Puffer talked louder.

"I can even ***prove*** it," he said. "Didn't you ever wake up with a **drool spot** on your pillow?"

I thought very hard.

"Yeah . . . so?"

"So where do you think it came from?" he asked. "It came from the *monster* under your bed, that's where. It was *monster* drool, Junie B. Jones."

I shook my head real fast.

"No it was not, Paulie Allen Puffer! You stop saying that! And I **mean** it!"

He raised up his **eyebrows**.

"Well, where did it come from then? *You* don't drool on your pillow. Do you? You're not a *baby*, are you?" he said.

"No! Don't call me that! I am not a baby!" I **yell**ed.

Paulie Allen Puffer **cross**ed **his arms**.

"So where did the drool come from then?" he asked again.

"I don't know," I said. "But my daddy told me there's no such things as monsters."

"So what? Daddies *have* to say that," said Paulie Allen Puffer. "That's so you'll go to sleep at night and not **bother** them."

He **squint**ed his eyes at me.

"Why do you think daddies and mommies sleep together in the same room, anyway? It's so they can *protect* each other from the monster. Or else their heads might get **chew**ed off."

Just then, I **wrinkle**d up my nose at that terrible thought. Then I hanged out my **tongue**. And I did a sick face.

And guess what?

The cheese man took the class picture.

2
Just Say *Right!*

After school pictures, we went back to Room Nine.

I put my head down on my table.

"There's no such things as **monster**s. There's no such things as monsters," I **whisper**ed to just myself. "'Cause my very own daddy told me that. And he wouldn't even lie to me . . . probably."

Mrs. said for me to sit up in my chair.

She passed out work for us to do.

It was called **print**ing our letters. Only I didn't actually feel like doing that.

I **tap**ped on my bestest friend named Lucille.

"Guess what, Lucille? There's no such things as monsters. There's really, really not. And so a monster doesn't even live under my bed, probably. Right, Lucille? Right? Right?"

"Shh! I'm doing my letters," she said.

"Yes, Lucille. I *know* you are doing your letters. Only I just wanted to tell you about the monster. 'Cause he's not even real . . . right?"

Lucille didn't say *right*.

"How come you're not saying *right*,

Lucille? Just say *right*. Okay? Just say *monsters aren't real*. And I won't even **bother** you anymore."

All of a sudden, Lucille did a mad breath.

"*Now* look what you made me do, Junie B.! You made me **ruin** my big G! I *told* you not to bother me!"

She quick **grab**bed her paper and runned[1] to Mrs. to fix it.

I tapped my fingers on my table.

Then I turned around and looked behind me.

I smiled at a boy named **crybaby**

---

1 **runned** (ran) 영어권 국가의 아이들이 동사의 과거형을 말할 때 모든 단어의 끝에 '-ed'를 붙이는 실수를 종종 한다. 이 책에 나오는 'springed(sprang)', 'freezed(froze)' 등이 이와 같은 경우이다.

William.

"Guess what, William. There's no such things as monsters. And so a monster doesn't even live under my bed, probably. Right? William? Right? Right?"

William moved his seat away from me.

I followed him in my chair.

"I'm right, don't you think, William? A monster really *doesn't* live under my bed, does he? Plus also, he doesn't put my head in his mouth."

William **slide**d his chair away some more.

I **scoot**ed after him.

"Just say *right*. Okay, William? Just say there's not a monster under my bed. And I will be **on my way**."

William picked up his chair. He carried it **all the way** to the middle of the floor.

That's how come I had to carry my chair to the middle of the floor, too.

I sat down and smiled very sweet.

"Right, William? I'm right, aren't I?" I said.

Only too bad for me. 'Cause just then I felt hands on my **shoulder**s.

I looked up.

It was Mrs.

I did a **gulp**.

"Hello. How are you today?" I said kind of nervous.

Mrs. **zoom**ed my chair back to my table.

It was not fun.

I quick picked up my pencil.

"Guess what? I am going to do my work now," I said. "Plus also, I am not even going to talk. 'Cause I don't actually like anyone in this area."

Mrs. tapped her foot at me.

"Love your shoes," I said real soft.

Her foot kept tapping.

Only just then, a very great thing happened. And it is called, the bell rang for the end of school!

I hurried up out the door.

Then me and my other bestest friend named Grace runned to the bus together.

"Grace! Grace! Guess what? There's no such things as monsters! And so I don't even have one under my bed, probably. Right, Grace? Right?"

That Grace didn't say *right*.

That's how come I grabbed her by her shoulders. And I **jiggle**d and jiggled her. 'Cause I was **fed up with** these people, that's why.

"How come you won't say *right*, Grace?

How come nobody will say *right?* 'Cause I'm getting **at the end of my rope** with this thing!"

That Grace took my hands off of her.

"I can't say *right,* because a monster really *might* live under your bed, Junie B.," she said.

My eyes got big and wide at her.

"No, Grace! No! Do not say that! Do not say a monster might live under my bed! 'Cause that cannot even be true. Or else I would have **spot**ted that guy by now!"

"No, you wouldn't," she said. "My big sister said that monsters can turn theirselves **invisible** when you look at them. And so that's how come nobody ever sees them."

That Grace looked serious at me.

"That **make**s **sense**, don't you think? Huh, Junie B.? Right?"

Just then, my **throat** got dry. And my **stomach** got the shakies.

I looked out the window very **upset**.

And I didn't say *right*.

3
The Invisiblest[1] Guy

I ran in my house and **holler**ed for my grandma Helen Miller.

"GRANDMA MILLER! GRANDMA HELEN MILLER! I AM SO GLAD TO BE HOME! 'CAUSE TODAY WAS NOT A VERY GOOD DAY AT MY SCHOOL!"

---

1 **invisiblest** 형용사 'invisible'의 최상급을 잘못 만든 것으로, 원래는 단어 'invisible'이 '보이지 않는'이라는 의미를 나타내기 때문에 형용사의 비교급이나 최상급으로 쓰지 않는다.

Grandma Miller was in the kitchen. She was holding my baby brother named Ollie.

I jumped up and down in front of her.

"PICK ME UP! PICK ME UP! PICK ME UP!"

"I can't right now, Toots,[2]" she said. "I've got my hands full with Ollie."

"Yeah, only put him on the floor," I said. "'Cause I need a **hug** down here, Helen."

Grandma Miller **lean**ed down and hugged me.

She said don't call her Helen.

"Why don't you go change your clothes?" she said. "Then you and I will

---

2 **toots** '아가씨'라는 뜻으로 애정을 담아 장난스럽게 어린 여성을 부르는 표현.

make some popcorn. And you can tell me all about your day. How does that sound?"

Just then, my whole face got happy. 'Cause popcorn is my most favorite[3] thing in the whole wide world!

"**Hurray**!" I shouted. "Hurray for popcorn!"

I ran right to my room. Then I took off my shoes and socks. And my feet did a happy dance on the floor. It was called the Happy Feet Popcorn Dance.

They danced around and around. Also, they jumped on my bed. And they **spring**ed to the floor. And they did a **giant**

---

3 **most favorite** '가장 좋아하는'이라는 뜻을 지닌 비격식적인 표현. 원래는 단어 'favorite'이 '선호하는'이라는 의미를 나타내기 때문에 형용사의 최상급을 만드는 부사인 'most'를 잘 붙이지 않는다.

twirly[4] on my **rug**.

I **clap**ped my hands real **joyful**.

"Grandma! Hey, Grandma! Guess what? I am having a good time in here! And so I am not even thinking about the monster under my bed!"

Just then, I did a **gulp**.

'Cause I shouldn't have said that, I think.

I looked at my bed kind of nervous.

What if the monster was under there right this very minute?

And what if he was looking at my **piggy toe**s?

And what if he wanted to *eat* them?

"Oh no," I said. "Oh no. Oh no. 'Cause

---

4 **twirly** 주니 B.가 만들어 낸 말로 단어 'twirl(빙글빙글 돌다)'의 뒤에 '-y'를 붙여 '빙글빙글 돌기'라는 의미의 명사로 사용하였다.

piggy toes look just like little wiener sausages,[5] I think."

I **freeze**d right where I was standing.

"GRANDMA MILLER! GRANDMA MILLER! COME QUICK! I NEED YOU!" I shouted.

Grandma Miller flied to my room. Then she picked me up. And she hugged me real tight.

"What on *earth* is the trouble?" she asked.

She sat down with me on my bed.

"NO, GRANDMA! NO! NO! WE CAN'T SIT HERE!"

I **squeeze**d out of her arms and ran out

---

5 **wiener sausage** 비엔나소시지. 손가락같이 가늘고 짧은 소시지. 쇠고기나 돼지고기로 만들며, 오스트리아 빈에서 처음 시작되었다고 한다.

my door.

"THERE'S A MONSTER UNDER MY BED!" I **yell**ed.

I jumped up and down.

"RUN, HELEN! RUN LIKE THE WIND!"

Only Grandma Helen Miller didn't run. She just **flop**ped back on my **cover**s. And she closed her eyes.

"No, Junie B. *Please*. We're not going to go through this monster business again, are we? We've talked about monsters before, remember? We decided that there are no such things as monsters."

"Yes, but I have new information," I said. "'Cause the monster under my bed turns himself invisible whenever we look at him. Plus at night—after my eyes are closed—he climbs next to me. And he puts my head in his mouth."

Grandma Miller did a big breath. Then she went to the kitchen. And she brought back my daddy's **flashlight**.

She shined it under my bed.

"No monster, Junie B. *None*. I don't see one single monster under this bed," she said.

"See?" I said. "That **prove**s it, Grandma! He turned himself invisible!"

Grandma Miller shook her head.

"No, Junie B. The monster did *not* turn himself invisible. The monster is simply not *there*. He does not *exist*. **Period**."

"Yes, he does, Grandma! He does *too*

exist. 'Cause Paulie Allen Puffer's big brother even said so. Plus also I've seen the **drool**."

Grandma Miller said to **calm** down my voice. She got me a drink of water.

"Why don't we forget about the monster for now, and we'll go make popcorn. You can talk to your mother about this when she gets home. I **bet** Mother will know **exact**ly what to do."

I thought and thought.

"What, Grandma? What will she do?" I asked.

Then—all of a sudden—a **light bulb went on** in my head.

"Hey! *I* know what she'll do! Mother will get the **broom** and **bash** the monster's head in! 'Cause I saw her do that to a **roach** before! And she is excellent at it!"

Grandma Miller closed her eyes again.

She said I am a strange one.

4
Spooky and Scary

Pretty soon, Mother came home from work.

I **zoom**ed to her **speedy** quick. And handed her the **broom**.

"MOTHER! MOTHER! COME ON! COME ON! LET'S GO! LET'S GO GET THE **MONSTER**!" I **holler**ed.

Mother turned her head real slow. And she looked at Grandma Miller.

Grandma **suck**ed in her **cheek**s.

"A monster," she said kind of quiet. "Under the bed. We've been waiting for you to come home, so you can **bash** its head in."

I **tug**ged on her sweater.

"Plus tell her about the drool, Grandma!" I said.

But Grandma Miller headed to the door. And she said the words *I'm outta here.*

I pulled on Mother's arm.

"Come on! Come on, Mother! The monster's really real! 'Cause Paulie Allen Puffer told me everybody has a monster under the bed! Plus that Grace said it can turn *invisible.* And so that is how come we never saw that guy before."

Mother sat down at the kitchen table. And she **lift**ed me onto her **lap**.

Then she said that Paulie Allen Puffer was just trying to **scare** me. Plus that Grace didn't know what she was talking about.

"There is *no* monster under your bed, Junie B. I promise you. Monsters are *not* real," she said.

"Yes, they are! They are too real! 'Cause Paulie Allen Puffer's brother even said so! And he is in seventh **grade**! And he said monsters **crawl** on your bed! And they **fit** your head in their mouth! And so that is where the drool comes from! 'Cause I am not even a baby!"

Just then, I heard the front door open.

It was my daddy! He was home from

work, too!

"Daddy, Daddy! There's a monster under my bed! Only you said monsters aren't real. But they really, really are!"

I pulled on his arm.

"Come on, Daddy! Let's get him!"

Daddy looked at Mother a real long time.

They went in the **hall** and did **whisper**ing.

Pretty soon, Daddy came back to me.

He said we would look for the monster after dinner. But first we would cook some hamburgers on the **grill**.

"Oh boy![1]" I said. "Oh boy! 'Cause

---

1 **boy** 여기에서는 '소년'이라는 뜻이 아니라, '맙소사' 또는 '어머나'라는 의미로 놀람이나 기쁨 등을 나타내는 표현으로 쓰였다.

hamburgers are my most favorite things in the whole wide world! Plus also I like pasketti[2] and meatballs.[3]"

After that, me and Daddy went outside.

He got a **flipper**[4] for the hamburgers. Then he gave me a flipper, too. 'Cause I am old enough, that's why.

I runned all over with that thing.

I flipped a rock and a flower and a **dirt** ball. Plus also, I flipped a dead **lizard** I found in the **driveway**.

Then Mother took my flipper away.

---

2 **pasketti** 영어권 국가의 어린아이들이 흔히 하는 실수로, 'spaghetti(스파게티)'를 잘못 말한 것이다.

3 **meatball** 미트볼. 곱게 다진 고기에 양파, 빵가루, 달걀 등을 넣고 반죽하여 작게 빚은 후 밀가루와 달걀을 입혀 튀기거나 구워 낸 서양식 요리.

4 **flipper** 요리 도구인 'spatula(뒤집개)'를 단어 'flip(홱 뒤집다)'을 사용하여 잘못 말한 것이다. 원래 'flipper'는 '지느러미' 또는 '오리발'이라는 뜻을 나타낸다.

'Cause I am not old enough, that's why.

After dinner I took my bath.

Then Mother and Daddy read me a story. And they **hug**ged me good night.

"See you in the morning," said Mother.

"See you in the morning," said Daddy.

I sat up in my bed.

"Yeah, only I can't even sleep in here. 'Cause you guys didn't bash that monster yet."

Daddy **rub**bed his tired eyes.

"There's *no* monster, Junie B. There is *nothing* to be afraid of," he said.

Then he kissed me. And he went out of my room. And Mother went with him.

I quick got out of bed and followed those two.

They turned around and **spot**ted me.

"Hello. How are you today?" I said very **pleasant**. "I am going to sit in the kitchen and not **bother** anyone. Plus also, I might watch **Eyewitness** News at Ten.[5]"

Mother carried me back to bed.

I followed her out again.

"Want to **bake** a lemon pie? A lemon pie would be fun, don't you think?" I asked.

This time, Mother **march**ed me back to my room real fast.

"Do *not* get up again, Junie B.," she said. "Enough is enough."

I waited for her feet to walk away.

Then I **tip**py-**toe**d to my baby brother's room. And I climbed into his **crib**.

It was very **crowd**ed in there.

---

5 **Eyewitness News at Ten** 가상의 뉴스 프로그램의 이름. 'Eyewitness News'는 기자 등이 현장에서 소식을 생중계하는 뉴스 진행 방식을 말한다.

That's how come I had to get out and put baby Ollie on the floor.

Then I climbed in his crib again. And I pulled up the **blanket** all warm and **cozy**.

Only too bad for me, 'cause just then that **crybaby** baby started to **scream**.

Daddy runned into the room speedy quick.

He turned on the light and saw me.

I did a gulp.

"Hello. How are you today?" I said kind of nervous. "I am all warm and cozy."

Daddy quick **swish**ed me out of there.

Then he put baby Ollie back in the crib.

And he took me to my bed again.

"Okay. **This is *it*,**" he **grouch**ed. "This is the *last* time I want to have to come in

here. Do you understand, missy?[6] Do *not* get out of this bed *one more time*."

I started to cry a **teeny** bit.

6 **missy** '아가씨'라는 뜻으로 화나 애정을 담아 어린 여성을 부르는 표현.

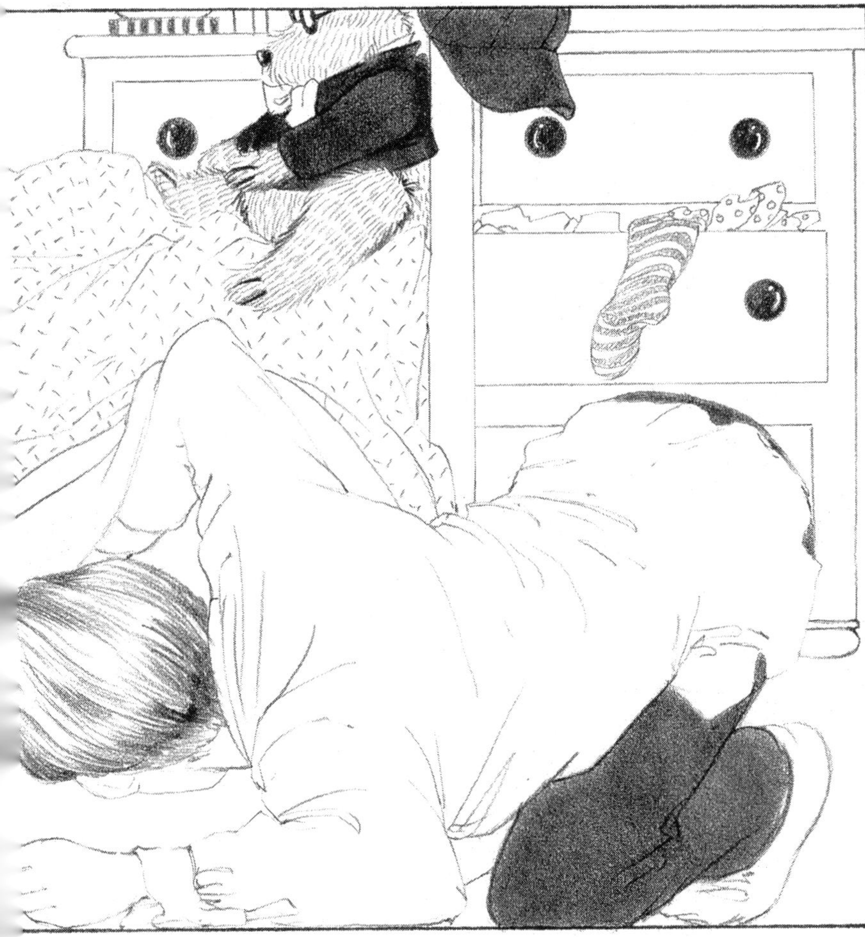

"Yeah, only what about the monster?" I said. "'Cause he is still under my bed, I think."

Daddy throwed his hands in the air. Then he turned on my light. And he looked for the monster all over the place.

First, he looked under my bed. Then he looked in my **closet**. And in my **drawers**. And in my **trash** can. Plus also, he looked in my crayon[7] box.

"*No* monster, Junie B.," he said. "No monster anywhere. You're going to have to believe me. Monsters are *not* real!"

He sat down on my bed.

"I'm going to go now," he said. "I'm going to leave your door open. And I'm going to leave the hall light on. But this is it, okay? You have to trust me, Junie B. There is *no* monster under your bed."

I holded onto his shirt.

---

7 **crayon** 크레용. 그림을 그릴 때 사용하는 연필 모양의 채색 도구. 안료에 파라핀 등을 섞은 후 녹여서 만든다.

"Yeah, only **tuck** in my **sheet**s. Okay? Tuck them in real tight. Or else my feet might hang over the side. And **piggy toe**s look like little wiener sausages."

Daddy tucked in my sheets. "There. Now good night."

"Yeah, only get my teddy.[8] Okay, Daddy? Plus also get my **Raggedy** Ann[9] named Ruth. And my Raggedy Andy[9] named Larry. And get my **stuff**ed elephant named Philip Johnny Bob."

Daddy got all those guys for me. He tucked them in my bed.

---

8 **teddy** 어린아이들이 장난감 곰 인형 테디 베어(teddy bear)를 부를 때 사용하는 애칭.

9 **Raggedy Ann, Raggedy Andy** 래기디 앤과 래기디 앤디. 또는 누더기 인형 앤과 앤디로 불린다. 미국의 작가 조니 그루엘(Johnny Gruelle)이 쓴 동화에 등장하는 남매 주인공이다. 빨간 실로 된 머리카락과 세모 모양의 코를 지닌 봉제 인형의 모습을 하고 있는 것이 특징이다.

"There. **That's *it***. Now good night," he said.

He walked right out of my room. And he kept on going down the hall.

I looked all around in the dark.

It was spooky and scary in there.

"PHILIP JOHNNY BOB WANTS A DRINK OF WATER!" I shouted out real loud.

I waited and waited.

"YEAH, ONLY HE REALLY, REALLY NEEDS ONE! **ON ACCOUNT OF** HE IS HAVING A PROBLEM WITH HIS **TRUNK!**"

Daddy didn't come.

"RAGGEDY RUTH NEEDS A KLEENEX![10]" I yelled next.

After that, my voice got quieter.

"Raggedy Larry wants a cookie," I said.

But still Daddy didn't come.

---

10 **Kleenex** 크리넥스. 본래 휴지나 기저귀 등을 판매하는 미국의 생활용품 브랜드의 이름이지만, 화장지를 일컫는 일반적인 용어로 굳어졌다.

5
My Worstest Night Ever

It was my worstest night ever.

I did**n't sleep** any **wink**s.

That's because I had to keep my eyes open. Or else the monster wouldn't stay **invisible**.

I heard Mother and Daddy go to bed.

"GOOD NIGHT, EVERYBODY! GOOD NIGHT! IT'S ME! IT'S JUNIE B. JONES! I AM STILL AWAKE IN HERE. 'CAUSE I

CAN'T EVEN CLOSE MY EYES OR THE MONSTER WILL COME!"

Mother and Daddy didn't **yell** back.

"PLUS HERE'S ANOTHER THING I NEED TO TELL YOU! DON'T TURN OUT THE **HALL** LIGHT. PLUS DON'T SHUT MY DOOR! PLUS DON'T SHUT YOUR DOOR, EITHER!"

"Go to sleep!" **grouch**ed Mother.

I smiled very **relieve**d.

"It was good to hear your voice," I said kind of quiet.

After that, Mother and Daddy got in bed. And they turned out their light.

Daddy started to **snore**.

"Oh no," I said. "Now he won't even be awake to save me if the monster comes."

I pulled Philip Johnny Bob out of my **cover**s.

"I will save you," he said. *"I will* ***squirt*** *water in the monster's face. Plus I will* ***stomple***[1] *him with my* **giant** *elephant feet. And so now you can close your eyes. And you don't even have to worry about that guy."*

I looked and looked at him.

"Yeah, only here's the problem," I said. "You're not actually strong 'cause you just have **fluffy**[2] in you. Plus also you can't really squirt water. And so who am I **kid**ding here?"

Philip Johnny Bob **stare**d at me a real

---

1 **stomple** '쿵쿵거리며 짓밟다'라는 뜻으로 주니 B.가 'stomp(쿵쿵거리며 걷다)'와 'trample(밟아 뭉개다)'을 합쳐 만들어 낸 말.

2 **fluffy** 단어 'fluff(솜털)'를 주니 B.가 'fluffy'라고 장난스럽게 말한 것이다.

long time.

Then he went back under the covers.

All of a sudden I heard feet in the hall.

It was monster feet, I think!

They kept getting closer and closer to me.

Then pretty soon they runned right in my room!

And guess what?

It was my dog, Tickle! That's what!

"Tickle! Tickle! I am so glad to see you! 'Cause now you can protect me from the monster! And so why didn't I think of this before?"

I pulled back my covers and **pat**ted for him to jump up.

"Here, Tickle! You can sleep right on my

pillow! 'Cause Mother won't even find out about this!"

Tickle **spring**ed right up there. He runned all around on my bed.

He put his head under my **sheet**s and runned down to my feet.

"No, Tickle! No! No! You have to come back up here! Or else how will you even protect me?"

I pulled him back up.

He put his **paw**s on **Raggedy** Larry. And **chew**ed his red hair.

"No, Tickle! No! No!" I said.

Just then, Tickle springed over me. And he **land**ed on my elephant named Philip Johnny Bob.

He holded him by his **trunk**. And

shaked that guy all around.

I saved Philip Johnny Bob just **in time**.

Then I pushed Tickle off my bed. And he runned out of my room.

Philip Johnny Bob was very **upset**.

I **pet**ted his trunk.

Also, I hugged Raggedy Larry.

Only too bad for me. 'Cause just then Raggedy Ruth fell right out of my bed. **On account of** the **dumb** sheets weren't **tuck**ed in anymore.

Me and Raggedy Larry **peek**ed over the side at her.

"Get her," said Raggedy Larry.

"Yeah, only I *can't* get her," I said real upset. "Or else the monster will **grab** my hand and pull me right under the bed."

I thought about what to do.

Then—all of a sudden—I picked up all my friends in my arms.

"We have to **make a run for it**," I told them. "We have to sleep with Mother and Daddy tonight. 'Cause we will be safe with them. Plus they won't even know we're there probably. 'Cause their bed is the size of a king."

I stood on the side of my bed. Then I jumped way out to the middle of the floor. And I quick picked up Raggedy Ruth.

I ran to Mother and Daddy's room.

They were sleeping and snoring.

"Shh," I said to Raggedy Larry.

"Shh," I said to Philip Johnny Bob.

Then all of us crawled down the middle

of their bed. And we **sneak**ed under their covers.

Only too bad for me. 'Cause Mother **roll**ed right over on Philip Johnny Bob's trunk. And it waked her right up.

She turned on the light.

I did a **gulp**.

"Hello. How are you today? Me and my friends are sleeping here. 'Cause we didn't think you'd mind, probably."

Mother carried me back to my room zippity[3] quick.

Then she **lean**ed close to my ear. And she talked very **scary** with her teeth closed.

---

3 **zippity** 단어 'zippy(아주 빠른)'를 강조하여 말한 것으로, 'zippity quick'은 '아주 빠르게'라는 뜻의 비격식적 표현이다.

"Do . . . *not* . . . get . . . out . . . of . . . bed . . . one . . . more . . . time," she said.

And so guess what?

I didn't.

6
Flatsos[1]

The next day at school, I was **pooped** and tired.

I opened one eye with my fingers. And I drawed a picture for art.

It did not **turn out** that **professional**.

After that, I holded up my head with my hands. And I waited for school to be over.

1 **flatso** 단어 'flat(납작한)'을 강조하여 말한 것으로, 본 책에서는 '납작이'로 번역했다.

Me and that Grace **rode** home on the bus together.

I **yawn**ed and yawned.

"Darn it,[2] Grace. I wish you never even told me that **monster**s can turn **invisible**. 'Cause now I can't even close my eyes at night."

"I can," said that Grace. "That's because I don't have a monster under my bed anymore. My mom **figure**d **out** how to **get rid of** it."

My eyes got big and wide.

"How, Grace? How did she do that?"

"Easy," said that Grace. "First, she **suck**ed it up in the **vacuum cleaner**. Then

---

2 **darn it** 'damn it(빌어먹을, 제기랄)'을 순화한 단어로, 못마땅하거나 짜증스러울 때 쓰는 속어적 표현.

she put the vacuum cleaner bag in the **trash compact**or. And she **squish**ed the monster into a *flatso.*"

Just then, I **hug**ged and hugged that girl! 'Cause that was **brilliant**, of course!

"Thank you, Grace! Thank you! Thank you! 'Cause I have a vacuum cleaner right in my very own home! And so I can do that too, probably!"

After I got off my bus, I **zoom**ed to my house **speedy** fast.

"GRANDMA MILLER! GRANDMA MILLER! I KNOW HOW TO GET RID OF THE MONSTER!" I **holler**ed.

Then I runned to the **closet** and got Mother's vacuum cleaner. And I pulled that big thing **all the way** to my room.

Grandma Miller came to my door.

I told her all about how to get rid of the monster. And guess what? She was a good **sport** about it!

First, she **plug**ged the vacuum cleaner right into my wall. Then she put it under the bed. And she sucked the monster right out of there!

"**HURRAY**! HURRAY! YOU GOT HIM! YOU GOT THE MONSTER, GRANDMA!" I yelled real **thrill**ed.

Grandma Miller runned with the bag to the kitchen. And she throwed it in the trash can.

"There. That ought to **do the trick**," she said very happy.

I looked and looked at the trash.

Then I did a **teeny frown**.

"Yeah, only here's the problem, Grandma. You didn't actually put the bag in the trash compactor. And that is what turns the monster into a flatso."

Grandma Miller smiled.

"Yes, but this house doesn't *have* a trash compactor, Junie B.," she said. "*Your* monster will just have to stay in the vacuum cleaner bag."

My frown got bigger.

"Yeah, but what if he **leak**s out, Grandma? Then maybe he might **float** in the air. All the way back to my room. And he will get under my bed again."

Grandma Miller **tap**ped on the **counter** with her fingers. Then her **cheek**s filled up with air. And she let it out real slow.

"Okay . . . how 'bout this? What if I take it outside? I'll take the bag outside. And I'll push it way down in the big **garbage** can. And then I'll **press** the **lid** down really tight, so he can't get out."

"Yeah, but he still won't be a flatso," I said very **whining**.

Just then, Grandma Miller got **fusstration** in her.

She grabbed the vacuum cleaner bag and ran outside.

Then she put it on the **driveway**.

And she got in her car.

And she backed up over that thing with her tires.

Pretty soon, she came back in the

house.

She **brush**ed her hands together.

"There! *Now* he's a flatso!" she said kind of **growly**.

After she left, I got on the **couch**. And I **stare**d very nervous at the driveway.

'Cause guess why?

A car is not a trash compactor.

That's why.

7
Snarlies and Snufflies

That night, I heard snarlies under my bed.

Mother said it was my **'magination**.

"No, it is *not* my 'magination," I said. "I can hear snarlies. Plus also I hear **snorie**s and snufflies and **drool**ies."

Mother **roll**ed **her eyes** way up at the **ceiling**.

"**Honest**ly, Junie B. . . . where in the *world* do you get this **stuff**?" she asked.

I thought and thought.

"It just **automatic**ally comes in my head," I said. "It is a **gift**, I think."

After that, I **beg**ged to sleep in her bed.

But Mother said no.

Then Daddy said no, too.

"You have to trust us, Junie B.," he said. "We would never let anything hurt you. There's nothing in your room to be afraid of."

And so that's how come I had to sleep in my own bed. For the whole **entire** night.

Plus also, I had to sleep there the next night. And the next night. And the next night after that, too.

That was the night when the worst thing of all happened.

'Cause I **accidental**ly sleeped too much. And the monster must have **crawl**ed on my bed. 'Cause in the morning there was drool on my **pillow**!

I **scream**ed very loud when I felt it.

"HELP! HELP! THERE'S DROOL! THERE'S DROOL! I *TOLD* YOU THIS WOULD HAPPEN! I *TOLD* YOU THE MONSTER WOULD COME!"

I ran in Mother and Daddy's room and showed them my pillow.

Mother holded her head.

"When is this *ever* going to end?" she said. "When are you *ever* going to **realize** that there are *no such things* as monsters?"

She did not wait for me to answer.

"*Everyone* drools on their pillow

sometimes," she said. "It doesn't mean you're a baby. Your mouth just opens when you're sleeping. And you drool a little bit. It's **no big deal**. And it is *not* from monsters!"

After that, she went out of her room to the kitchen. And Daddy went to get Ollie.

I crawled into her bed and **count**ed my **piggy toe**s.

Good news.

There was ten.

That day at **kindergarten**, Mrs. had a surprise for us.

It was called our school pictures were back from the cheese man.

She passed them out to us.

Lucille got hers first.

My eyes **pop**ped out at those things!

"Lucille! Look how **gorgeous** they are! They are the gorgeousest[1] pictures I ever saw!" I said.

Lucille **fluff**ed her **fluffy** dress.

"I know it. I know they are gorgeous.

---

1 **gorgeousest** 형용사 'gorgeous'의 최상급을 잘못 만든 것으로, 올바른 표현은 'most gorgeous'이다.

That's just how I look, Junie B. I can't even help it."

After that, Lucille stood up at the table. And she held up her pictures for everyone to see.

Mrs. said *sit down* to her.

Just then, Mrs. **bend**ed down next to me. And she **smooth**ed my hair.

"Junie B., honey? You might want to have *your* pictures taken again," she said kind of quiet.

Then she handed me my **envelope** real secret. So nobody could see.

I **sneak**ed a **peek** at those things.

My **stomach** felt **sickish** inside.

"I look like I smelled **stink**," I said.

I quick tried to hide my pictures. But Lucille **grab**bed them away from me.

"Eeew! **Gross**!" she said. "Junie B. looks

gross!"

I tried to grab them back.

"YEAH, ONLY THESE ARE NOT EVEN YOUR BEESWAX,[2] MADAM![3]"

---

2 **beeswax** '일' 또는 '용무'라는 뜻으로 'not your business(당신이 신경 쓸 일이 아니다)'와 같은 표현에서 발음이 유사한 business를 좀 더 부드럽게 말할 때 사용한다.

3 **madam** '계집애'라는 뜻으로 건방진 여자아이를 얕잡아 부를 때 사용하는 비격식적인 호칭.

I **yell**ed very mad.

Only too bad for me. 'Cause lots of other kids already saw them. And they laughed and laughed at those things.

Finally I grabbed the pictures back. And I hided them in my coat.

I didn't talk to Room Nine for the whole rest of the day.

8
Scary-face Me!

After I got home from school, I sat on my bed. And I looked at my pictures.

"I hate these ugly, **dumb** things!" I said very **furious**. "These are the ugliest dumb pictures I ever even saw!"

I **lean**ed over the **edge** and holded a picture down there.

"See this? See this, you stupid **monster**? This picture is just as scary as you! And so maybe I might put it right under my bed! And it will **scare** your whole **entire** pants off!"

Just then, I sat up very straight.

'Cause that might be a good idea I just thought of!

I quick found my scissors.

Then I cut my school pictures apart from each other. And I **shove**d them right under my bed.

"I am not even afraid of you, you dumb monster! 'Cause these ugly pictures can **bite** your head off!"

Just then, I heard Mother come home from work.

"Mother! Mother! My pictures came! My pictures came!" I **holler**ed very

thrilled.

She hurried up to my room.

I pointed under my bed.

"See them, Mother? See my school pictures? I **spread** them out under there."

Mother looked **curious** at me.

She **bend**ed down and picked up a picture.

Her mouth did a **gasp**.

"Oh my," she **whisper**ed.

I **clap**ped and clapped.

"I know they are *oh my!* That is why I put them under my bed! Get it, Mother? Get it? Now my scary face will be down there all the time! And so that monster already got scared away, I **bet**!"

All of a sudden, Mother started to laugh.

Then I started to laugh, too.

Plus here's another happy thing. 'Cause this morning there was more **drool** on my **pillow**.

Only I am not that worried.

'Cause it was from **Raggedy** Ruth, I bet. Or else maybe it was from Philip Johnny Bob.

Or maybe it was even from me.

But that does not mean I'm a baby.

'Cause *everybody* drools on their pillow once in a while!

My very own mother told me that.

And she would not even lie to me . . .

probably.